Advance Praise for
SCORCHED EARTH

"A formally kaleidoscopic work that oscillates between history, family, friendship, love, and the vexed precarity of modern life, *Scorched Earth* both challenges and soothes at once. But what I love most about these poems, and in Tiana's poems at large, is the way they name and hold the archive, the barbed histories, the loved ones and the nemeses in our world, with such intelligent tenderness. Here, the ache of lived experience is recast, as it is in our most indelible poems, as sites of wonder and luminosity, where our wounds are—thank god—not merely subjects, but methods."

—Ocean Vuong, author of *On Earth We're Briefly Gorgeous*

"'I still want joy at the end,' Tiana Clark writes in *Scorched Earth*, her searing, expansive new collection of poems. This book *begins* with an end—the speaker's divorce—and the poems unpack what it means to have outlived the life you'd expected to have. 'If my body be a long poem,' Clark writes, 'then I want it to go wherever it needs.' These are poems of Black joy, queer love, and radical acceptance of the self. *Scorched Earth* is a hell of a book."

—Maggie Smith, *New York Times* bestselling author of *You Could Make This Place Beautiful*

"*Scorched Earth* is quite the title for this stunning volume in which Tiana Clark challenges our notions of just how many times a poem can turn and just how much any poem can hold. Each page reads as if it is hungry for understanding—of divorce, of Blackness, of the American South, of poetry itself: 'I want to peg / the canon. So I am running back / and forth between the house of silence / and the house of shame . . .' Clark's is an ever-evolving voice that we need to hear!"

—Jericho Brown, Pulitzer Prize–winning author of *The Tradition*

"I can give three reasons for why Tiana Clark is a great poet. One—her self-intimacy is really shocking and strong—and she *owns* it. Two—she knows where to stop (i.e., end the poem), she puts her finger on it, and it's true or it feels true. Ultimately, her poetry is one big safe word. That's three. It's crazy gorgeous, and it stops everything."

—Eileen Myles, author of *I Must Be Living Twice*

"To read *Scorched Earth* is to touch the electric fire of Tiana Clark's mind—crackling with visceral, wonderfully dangerous poems exploring the feminine erotic, she writes unapologetically about Black womanhood, sexuality, desire, and its mirror world of grief, doubt, and unbelonging. This collection is a celebration of the expense of Black femininity as its own cosmos of possibility. What a joy to see a poet write so deliciously toward longing, yearning, and, ultimately, her own incendiary self."

—Safiya Sinclair, author of *How to Say Babylon*

SCORCHED EARTH

SCORCHED EARTH

Poems by

Tiana Clark

WASHINGTON SQUARE PRESS

ATRIA

NEW YORK   AMSTERDAM/ANTWERP   LONDON   TORONTO   SYDNEY   NEW DELHI

WASHINGTON
SQUARE PRESS

ATRIA

An Imprint of Simon & Schuster, LLC
1230 Avenue of the Americas
New York, NY 10020

First Washington Square Press/Atria Paperback edition March 2025

WASHINGTON SQUARE PRESS/ATRIA PAPERBACK and colophon
are trademarks of Simon & Schuster, LLC

For information about special discounts for bulk purchases, please contact
Simon & Schuster Special Sales at 1-866-506-1949 or business@simonandschuster.com.

The Simon & Schuster Speakers Bureau can bring authors to your live event.
For more information or to book an event, contact the Simon & Schuster Speakers Bureau
at 1-866-248-3049 or visit our website at www.simonspeakers.com.

Interior design by Jason Snyder

Manufactured in the United States of America

1 3 5 7 9 10 8 6 4 2

Library of Congress Cataloging-in-Publication Data

Names: Clark, Tiana, author.
Title: Scorched earth / poems by Tiana Clark.
Other titles: Scorched earth (Compilation)
Description: First Washington Square Press/Atria edition. | New York :
Washington Square Press/Atria, 2024.
Identifiers: LCCN 2023050000 (print) | LCCN 2023050001 (ebook) | ISBN
9781668052075 (paperback) | ISBN 9781668052082 (ebook)
Subjects: LCGFT: Poetry.
Classification: LCC PS3603.L36925 S36 2024 (print) | LCC PS3603.L36925
(ebook) | DDC 811/.6—dc23/eng/20231027
LC record available at https://lccn.loc.gov/2023050000
LC ebook record available at https://lccn.loc.gov/2023050001

ISBN 978-1-6680-5207-5
ISBN 978-1-6680-5208-2 (ebook)

For my single mother,
who taught me first how to survive the ruins.

. . . I've been remembering the story of salt. Lot's wife.

But you tell me something the story never did:
Look back at the burning city. Still, live.

—ARACELIS GIRMAY

PROLOGUE

Then I know that there is room in me
for a second huge and timeless life.

—RAINER MARIA RILKE

Proof

I once made a diorama from a shoebox
for a man I loved. I was never a crafty person,

but found tiny items at an art store and did my best
to display the beginning bud of our little love,

a scene re-creating our first kiss in his basement
apartment, origin story of an eight-year marriage.

In the dollhouse section, I bought a small ceiling fan.
Re-created his black leather couch, even found minuscule

soda cans for the cardboard counters that I cut and glued.
People get weird about divorce. Think it's contagious.

Think it dirty. I don't need to make it holy, but it purifies—
it's clear. Sometimes the science is simple. Sometimes

people love each other but don't need each other
anymore. Though I think the tenderness can stay

(if you want it to). I forgive and keep forgiving,
mostly myself. People still ask, *What happened?*

I know you want a reason, a caution to avoid,
but life rarely tumbles out a cheat sheet. Sometimes

nobody is the monster. I keep seeing him for the first
time at the restaurant off of West End where we met

and worked and giggled at the micros. I keep seeing his
crooked smile and open server book fanned with cash

before we would discover and enter another world
and come back barreling into this one, astronauts

for the better and for the worse, but still spectacular
as we burned back inside this atmosphere to live

separate lives inside other shadow boxes we cannot see.
I remember I said *I hate you* once when we were driving

back to Nashville, our last long distance. I didn't mean it.
I said it to hurt him, and it did. I regret that I was capable

of causing pain. I think it's important to implicate
the self. The knife shouldn't exit the cake clean.

There is still some residue, some proof of puncture,
some scars you graze to remember the risk.

CONTENTS

I.

THERE IS STILL SOME RESIDUE

Self-Portrait at Divorce

The day my husband left
I accidentally set off the house alarm
and the dog finally curled into my chest
like a warm croissant of cream fur and you
had replaced the trash bag for the last time
and the recycling and I walked into
your office and I wept and wept inside
your pillow on our bed (whoops) I mean *my* bed
a California king *our* biggest bed yet because
we wanted space for *our* long bodies to stretch
and room for the dog to splay and I put water
in the dog bowl and I told myself that I had to remember
to do that because you had always done that simple task
and you often reminded me to do it when I forgot and I didn't
want *our* dog to die of thirst and you left a cup of water
on the end table by the couch we had picked out the year before—
we had just walked into an Ashley furniture store on a Saturday
and sat on the first fake living room set and said *this is us*
like we knew what we wanted but we did that day (we did)
and it was easy (which was rare for us)—and I put your last cup
of water to my mouth and I guessed where your mouth
might have been on the rim and I pressed my lips to the glass
(I had the nicest lips like two pillows you always said)
and I kissed the cup and poured out the rest of the water
into the sink and it wasn't an offering to anything and I put
the cup in the dishwasher and I started to tremble and the house
seemed (smelled?) like it was a train but it was just the actual train
that rumbles behind our house (I mean *my* house)
and you called and told me you went to the hospital
for chest pains and I wasn't with you at the walk-in clinic
but you said I was still your emergency contact

and I slept on the couch that night because I didn't want
to sleep in *our* (I mean) *my* big bed and I wanted to grovel *my* way
back to the complacency of us and I wanted to grasp at the stomach
of anyone and I wanted the almost-happy home we had
and I keep walking into each room and staring at the objects
that we bought together remembering fights at Target laughter
at Target splitting up and conquering a to-do list at Target
and those little zapper guns they gave us at Target when we
registered for our wedding gifts and I haven't showered
in days I have a sourness to me and the lids of my eyes
are swollen like tiny beige water balloons from all the sobbing
and I wanted to end this poem with gladness instead of the sound
of the knife drawer opening and closing opening and closing music
of metals and cabinet wood jingle and the clink of steel blades
and measuring spoons rustling against their edges and contours
and I didn't harm myself because I did want to harm myself I wanted
to feel the negotiation of pain besides the present pain and I wanted
the body's paint to come (but I didn't do it OKAY) I just thought
about it and I think I am proud of myself today for sitting down inside
the empty well of grief and looking up (I always forget to look up)
and *I didn't do it okay* I didn't and I still want joy at the end,
but the day my husband moved out it felt like the first real day
of fall because it was

I Like the Way Josh Says Black Love Is Radical

Tonight, I went to the park again,
because I couldn't stop crying. I don't

remember my dreams, and when I do
someone is always dying. Someone is always

grabbing my arm when I wake up. Once,
I woke to my own bite marks on my bicep.

Tonight, my friend Josh said he did not
exist in his own romantic imagination,

and I felt a zap of acknowledgment dip
through my chest like a tiny black bat

skittering the delicate lake for little bugs.
Tonight, I wanted to ask a better question

but couldn't, so I told Josh why I wanted
to live instead. Tonight, wherever the sunset

smeared the pink ghosts in the sky from dusk
to dust and other kinds of dreamy darknesses . . .

Tonight, I'll probably call my ex-husband
and say nothing, then hang up.

I'll open the fridge and say nothing too.
I'll take one more bite of tiramisu. What

a delightful word. You kind of have to sing to say it.

Self-Portrait at 35: Terror

I had a terror since September, I could tell to none; and so I sing,
as the boy does by the burying ground, because I am afraid.

—EMILY DICKINSON'S LETTER TO THOMAS
WENTWORTH HIGGINSON ON APRIL 26, 1862

Sometimes it's just easier to think about not existing, but I don't
make real plans to end it anymore. I just carry the passive

ideation with me like a black purse that's heavier than it looks,
leaving a red dent in my shoulder, a dark divot that only I can see.

I'm trying to quit coffee, because of my panic attacks, my anxiety,
my tendency to pace—not with my feet but with my racetrack mind.

My heartbeat, a squirrel's tail or a busybody squirrel scurrying up
a tree or a squirrel's beady eye catching mine and then darting away.

I know the little furry animal sees the frantic animal in me—terrified at 35,
not knowing anything about myself anymore, but still holding myself

> against the wake
> of all this unknowingness.

I take my coffee with heated heavy whipping cream, Brain Octane oil,
and vanilla monk fruit sweetener. Yes, I'm that extra and bougie

and always trying the next new fad. I'm so jittery and alert with my own
terrific black light, sipping. I've tried the imitation made with chicory

and roasted dandelion roots. It's weak, leaves me craving, dissatisfied.
I'm so tired of wanting more.

My Therapist Wants to Know about My Relationship to Work

I hustle
     upstream.
I grasp.
      I grind.
I control & panic. Poke
balloons in my chest,
always popping there,
always my thoughts thump,
thump. I snooze—wake & go
boom. All day, like this I short
my breath. I scroll & scroll.
I see what you wrote—I like.
I heart. My thumb, so tired.
My head bent down, but not
in prayer, heavy from the looking.
I see your face, your phone-lit
faces. I tap your food two times
for more hearts. I retweet.
I email: *yes & yes & yes.*
Then I cry & need to say: *no-no-no.*
Why does it take so long to reply?
I FOMO & shout. I read. I never
enough. New book. New post.
New ping. A new tab, then another.
Papers on the floor, scattered & stacked.
So many journals, unbroken white spines,
waiting. *Did you hear that new new?*
I start to text back. Ellipsis, then I forget.
I balk. I lazy the bed. I wallow when I write.
I truth when I lie. I throw a book

when a poem undoes me. I underline
Clifton: *today we are possible.* I start
from image. I begin with Phillis Wheatley.
I begin with Phillis Wheatley. I begin
with Phillis Wheatley reaching for coal.
I start with a napkin, receipt, or my hand.
I muscle memory. I stutter the page. I fail.
Hit delete—scratch out one more line. I sonnet,
then break form. I make tea, use two bags.
Rooibos again. I bathe now. Epsom salt.
No books or phone. Just water & the sound
of water filling, glory—be my buoyant body,
bowl of me. Yes, lavender, more bubbles
& bath bomb, of course some candles too.
All alone with Coltrane. My favorite, "Naima,"
for his wife, now for me, inside my own womb.
Again, I child back. I float. I sing. I simple
& humble. Eyes close. I low my voice,
was it a psalm? Don't know. But I stopped.

The Hardest Part of the Human Body

I want to love my teeth—

                their crooked city skyline
                and lemon-stained swagger.

Who wants to have a perfect smile?

                    I do and I don't.
        I need to stay humble

            on my knees

begging

      for some lover to notice

one unique feature

        about my face. The asymmetry, perhaps.

I lick my lips

        at the world. I know.

I know I shouldn't say

      I'm ugly,

            but what if I just whispered it

    to myself every now and then:

          I'm ugly. I'm ugly.

What if I say it

    when I pass a man

    who looks away from me,

    a man who might look like

        my father (but I've never seen my father).

And what if I say it before I eat,

      a simple prayer: *I'm ugly.*

        Say it instead of *hello,*

say it and say it

      until I become each inscrutable flaw,

      make a home for my pain with repetition.

I say *touch me*,

        touch me
        where I'm ugly,
        put your hands

                inside my mouth
                inside my wet teeth
                touch my crowns
                packed with porcelain
                slide your fingers
                around each uneven tooth
                touch my body

in the not-perfect places,
        tell me where I'm ugly,
            say my new name—
                tell me and touch and touch

—it doesn't hurt.
I take the word
the way I take a torso:
        sometimes a little bit,
            sometimes all at once.

Isn't it strange to be crammed
with what can   and cannot own you?

Pleasure toggles there   like a whistle of tired skin and juice.

A god told me I was ugly once
            and I believed and stared
at my hands, wishing
they were mirrors.
            I want to touch you
            like a mirror touches,
everywhere   at once.

A mirror can be a god
creating every shade and shape of hydrangea:
frothy ocean at dawn/open-throated pink bird/slate, then amethyst,

and then my mother's keys
opening the door
so little-poet-me
can fall asleep again.
No longer afraid
of what the dark
reanimates.

I flash my teeth
like a beast.

I want to end this
like you end
a dying ghazal
penned inside
my own howling—   Oh, Tiana, I want to love you there.

After the Plain Day Becomes Magnificent to Her

Someone I know is about to receive
a marriage proposal. It's January 30, 2021,
in Nashville, Tennessee. It's cold. It's Saturday.
It's still the pandemic. The weather spits
freezing rain, almost hail, but sadder. Sloppier?
Outside my window bare winter branches
beckon the soft white bulb in the sky diffused
in low relief. This day could be so ordinary,
could just slip by like a blip with just my laundry
folded and a few answered emails, but someone
I know is getting good news today, and I, with a
small group of people wearing masks, will wait
in her backyard after she says *yes*, after the plain day
becomes magnificent to her. We will coo and ogle
at her sparkling ring like cockatoos. I will rub
my thumb at the back of my ring finger where my
wedding ring used to be, a sapphire heated to a deep
and gleaming purple. My thumb will rub that little
pillow of skin underneath the knuckle, ghosting
the loss and the feeling of cool metal there,
but ultimately thankful. I stopped wearing my ring
long before my divorce, a foreshadow and then
the real shadow I had to confront and welcome
and wade through on my knees in supplication.
But I still believe in love, which is why I am bringing
her flowers from Amelia's, which is why she brought
me flowers from Amelia's when my divorce was final.
The card read, *Congratulations on taking a brave step!*
I think it all takes courage: falling in love, staying in love,
leaving love that no longer serves you, loving yourself—
No, I mean really loving yourself, really looking at yourself

in the mirror and accepting everything you see there,
your whole beautifully flawed body, drinking yourself
in like a lake in love with its wateriness, getting verbal
with it—you yourself saying, *I love you. I love you. I accept*
you exactly as you are right now. You are so easy to love. You are
so lovable and wonderful. It's astonishing, isn't it? Loving
yourself like that. But just now two cardinals darted
outside of my window while I was making black tea
with a giant squeeze from half of a fat lemon. I was
taking a quick break from writing this poem, and I
remember researching that cardinals mate for life   up!
and I think that's a good sign for today, especially   up and
for sweet Emily and Ben, a sweet day to celebrate   up and
your new rung in the ladder of love going up and up and

After the Reading

someone asked me if my husband left me, or if I left him. After the reading, someone asked me if there was a chance for reconciliation as I shoved a pulled pork sandwich in my mouth with Carolina Gold BBQ sauce oozing out the sides like neon yellow lava. After the reading, someone asked me if I still pray to God as I sipped a fizzy Diet Coke and the ice cubes huddled and softly clinked around my upper lip, leaving a wet mustache. After the reading, someone said they had been divorced too and then scurried away in a way that I completely understood. After the reading, a woman told me I was worthy, as if I was shattered, while I picked up crudités with a copious dollop of ranch dressing. After the reading, a white woman thanked me for my "angry poems." I told her they were about my joy, and then she touched my forearm and said, "No, they were about my rage." Insisting. After the reading, someone said they cried, and another gave me a kind word. Thank you. After the after, I went home and changed into my cheetah-print pajamas. I wrapped my hair and brushed my teeth. I got in bed and played a sci-fi show on my laptop. The actors on the show were trying to find a way to talk to aliens by using math and pheromones. I googled the height of one of the actors. He is 6'4". I fell asleep while watching the show about the people in space trying to communicate in first contact, intergalactic noises beeped and swirled around the room like bees.

II.

SOME PROOF OF PUNCTURE

The First Black Bachelorette

When Bryan was kissing Rachel
and slid his hand inside her hair, her long,
long hair, I wondered if he felt threaded
tracks of weave and what he thought
when he felt her weave. Was he startled
or did he know? But. When he reached
for her, I felt his fingers on my scalp too.
I did, through the TV, I swear! I was wincing.
My white guy doesn't like fake things, but I
like my fake hair long and my real hair protected,
my glory tucked and hidden. Something easy
and fast. I'm hoping it will grow too. I wonder
who does Rachel's hair on the show, blending
her "leave out" with her natural hair. Who slicks
her edges down with good grease and a boar brush
when the wind blows back her baby hairs?

~

There was an episode once
on *The Fresh Prince of Bel-Air*
with the actress Tisha Campbell.
The premise: they were on a date
and stuck in a basement for hours.
She stripped off her weave, fake nails,
contacts, and eyelashes. She molted.
Will then asks, *Now, what else*
on your body can I get at the mall?
RuPaul says, *We're all born naked*
and the rest is drag. Derrick has a list
of funny drag names and I want one.
I want to be called what I really am
or what I pretend to be, which, I guess,
in a way is me? Or someone who I think
might be beautiful enough to be approached,
discovered. Someone who doesn't have
to pay for movers. Someone who walks
into a party and doesn't have to be anxious
because the privilege of their beauty
makes them at rest and people find vacations
in their faces. I require something fake.
Woven and glued, stuck to my body
but not of my body. How does a body
even start?

~

Sometimes my eyes feel thick
and weird from fresh eyelash
extensions. In the beginning,
my head hurt from the braided
ropes of hair encircling my scalp,
tight. *But you want it tight*, she says.
You want the cornrows
so small that your fake
hair looks passable. In hope,
you take the pain. It takes
so damn long to be almost
beautiful. I've sat in salon chairs
all day with Black women behind me,
laboring and taming my mane.
I like the patterned crop circles carved
into my scalp right before the wefts
of somebody else's Brazilian hair are sewn
like human icing into mine, delicious.
I want the fire to smell a type of threat
in me and back away. I want the fire
to know I was already consumed,
burned inside my belonging.

~

There is a hankering.
A hungry choir that craves
money and porn, meaning
my thoughts are well lit,
staged, and faking it too.
Even my soul is pre-oiled,
fluffed, bleached, waxed,
nubile, licking, staring
down the camera to ash. The trick
is looking like you like it,
like you enjoy getting slammed,
which is why I like being groomed:
getting yanked, painted, cut,
and plucked. I've been on all fours
as a woman ripped me
from my center, where I split
in jeweled halves. I did not yell
as I bit my lip, grabbed the corners.
I enjoy how people look at me
when they think I might be beautiful.
I enjoy porn best when I think
they might be enjoying themselves too.
When there might be real pleasure
at stake, but who can say, really?
Not showing pain gets you paid.

~

And yet, Rachel.
Rachel, who scratches your dandruff
like Tea Cake in chapter eleven
of *Their Eyes Were Watching God*?
Who detangles and combs your hair
with deep conditioner? Who wraps
your hair at night? Has Bryan seen you
in your silk bonnet yet? You know
it's real when you're riding on top
with your hair wrapped. *It takes a lot*
of money to look this trashy, Dolly Parton
says. LaLa Milan says she was never ugly,
just poor. I want my teeth fixed and chiseled,
but veneers are so expensive. I hide
my coffee-stained crooked things.
Cardi B raps, *Got a bag and fixed*
my teeth. Hope you hoes know
it ain't cheap. So I try to hide
the unevenness in my teeth
when I talk, which means,
sometimes, I don't talk
when I can see myself. I try
to hide the gaps and how sharp
my teeth really are. How animal.
How lower-class. How cash-poor
my mouth really is. I don't look pretty
when I cum. My mouth, open. My jaw,
slack and sideways, pooling spit.
My deadened eyes fixed on one

object in the room. This time, a chair.
This time, a corner, half in shadow.
This time, I just wanted to watch
a Black woman on TV fall in love
for entertainment. For escape.
The best cure for microagressions
is shitty TV, and again, Cardi B.

~

Amaud says, for us, American Blacks,
we are postapocalyptic. The end
is not near but behind us. We are
what survived of our twelve million
enslaved, shipped, and spread. We are
what was not hung, dumped, or flung
from the *Zong*, splashing and graveless,
lest you think the ocean a tombstone.
The ocean is not scared or scared enough.
But. We out here! Anyway. Trying to save
ourselves, still. Still sprinkling black pepper
behind our feet as we run away. But. There is
no north now. We find the drinking gourd
within our cells. Guiding stars within
our own black-lit blood. We glow.
Maybe it is true, then. . .that beauty
is a type of survivor's guilt, a sackcloth
I suffer and itch and injure from and for.
Or, rather, that I am seen through sin?
Dirty Hottentot zoo is my body.

~

I was such a terrible Lady Macbeth
in high school. Her mania
didn't make sense to me
until it was activated in me
when a man left me in my blood
and twenties. There is a type
of grief I carry in my hands,
some dark, unwipeable
thought. Some liquid other.
Like my daddy's DNA. His spots.
I'm trying to cover them
with this talk of beauty.
I'm repenting for something—
I don't know what.
I wasn't meant to be born,
but ain't I a beautiful bastard?
And doesn't everybody
want to be cleaned
by slices of jailed light?
Yes, it's true,
I want my eyebrows
microbladed for $700.
There are specific times
when I don't want to be wanted:
1) At night. 2) When I'm alone.
3) At night, when I'm walking alone
to my car. 4) An empty parking lot.
5) A man approaches. 6) He sniffs me,

knowing that familiar scent
of pressure and piss
from other men
who have marked
me too. 7) Didn't they touch me
because I was beautiful?
Or did they sense
what was easy to poke?

~

I've always wondered
what made a slave beautiful
enough to be raped.
What about the body
made it worth it
to commit a sin
on what they deemed
a damned body.
Maybe beauty had nothing
to do with it. Of course, it's
always about power, but maybe
there was a type of sheen?
Lacquer on Black bodies
baking under sun?
Funk from the field?
The house slave
dilating from room
to room, a physiological
scent that niggles, perhaps?
How close desire is
to a type of terror,
owned and familiar.
When I get ready
with golden highlighter,
is this what I am . . .
what I accentuate?
My cheekbone
to sparkle in the spectral
light of my dead
belling inside me?
The sparkle of dead
slaves is forever in me,
still, so iridescent.

~

Keats wrote,
Beauty is truth, truth beauty,—that is all . . .
I don't know what that means.
I've had some dark inkling
about the succinct finality,
even in class I pretended
to know what the poem was about
when I would discuss ekphrasis
and the Grecian urn with my students,
telling them about art responding to art
and how to make a static image sing,
but even then, I was pretending.
I don't want to be dumb—
my worst fear: a bunch of students
would all point and call me a fraud.
I once asked Mark, my professor
in grad school, when I would stop
feeling like an impostor.
He said I would feel this way
for the rest of my life,
which I think is closer to some
type of truth, which is attractive,
because it provides relief
to know everyone might be
just as insecure and afraid of others
as me, and, possibly, watching
The Bachelorette on Monday nights,
like when I found out
on the podcast *Commonplace*
Sharon Olds loves the show too,
I squealed, because I wasn't alone
anymore.

~

I'm not writing
for mastery or legacy.
I couldn't care less.
In fact, I might be
writing against it,
a way of talking back
to beauty, back
to the spoiled fruit
on the altar of my body,
to the pressurized gaze
on my skin. Every. Damn.
Day. *I'm hyper-aware*
that I am hyper-visible,
says Hope Oloye, 20,
from Newham, East London,
the only Black biomedical student
in her year at Oxford.
Who hasn't been broken
by a touch? Who hasn't been barbed
by a glare? You can't write poems
about beauty when the streets are full
of racists and rapists and the president
is a pussy grabber. I want to peg
the canon. So I am running back
and forth between the house of silence
and the house of shame, shouting over
and over with ink-stained fingers,
On days when I write with duende
no one can touch me!

Scattered, Covered, & Smothered:
A Southern Gothic Sonnet

after and for Flannery O'Connor

I am pissing   in a bathroom   with pictures   of pickaninnies

lil' po' Blacks with lil' squiggles for hair squirming in a line for the outhouse

this pic   is supposed   to be funny   to someone   because the South

is absurd   near tragicomic   all I knew how to write   was my violence

I didn't know   it was possible   to transcend   it   my soft   slavebreaker

can you laugh   during a moment   of grace   I am starting   to lean

into the bleak   turn   as the car rolls   into a ditch   there's always

a black   hearse   a dark   forest at the fringe with   *Co'cola*

there is always   some hell-bent Misfit   drenched with dialect

I am not the racist   grandmother   but I might be the blood   splattered cat

rubbing glands against the shins   of my new owner spraying my niggerish scent

asking myself   what is a good man   why yo daddy so hard   to find

why you're one of my babies   she said   she ain't too proud to beg   but

anyone can be redeemed by a bullet   I wipe myself   & flush the toilet

50 Lines after *Figure* (2001) by Glenn Ligon

You know how it works when you make a photocopy
of a photocopy? The original fights to be seen
but appears blurred in each new version.

—MATTHEW OLZMANN

50 self-portrait poems

50 ghazals with "resilience" as the radif

50 broken sonnets with the same face as the volta

50 deleted lines about the pandemic (b/c I'm still processing it)

50 monostichs about Paul Robeson as Othello

50 love letters I write to a version of myself I want to believe isn't lying

50 witty out-of-office autoresponder email messages

50 frames, cabinets, and/or shadow boxes as anaphora

50 epigraphs from Gregory Pardlo that read, "The ekphrastic poet,
  that is to say all poets, must become an expert in the art of framing."

50 line breaks as tarot cards forecasting your face appearing and then disappearing again

50 end-stopped lines with em dashes

50 mug shots

50 contexts out of context

50 Glenn Ligons

50 Tiana Clarks

50 unmurdered Breonna Taylors

50 George Floyds coupled with joy and no knee on his neck, and yet

50 times I can't unsee your face as censored caesura

50 times I betrayed   and forgave myself   in the silent frame   caesura   holds

50 times I whispered, "Those who can afford to wait can wait without anxiety."

50 poems I burned in praise of nonattachment

50 selfies and/or layers of meaning and nonmeaning

50 obsessions when I looked to see who looked back at my Instagram story (ughhh)

50 figures of the same *almost* face—obscured—differently, each time a new background
color blooming inside 50 9 x 6" silk screen portraits

50 times a poem did and didn't make sense to me until it clicked in me—ya know?

50 revisions where I exhausted each surprise

50 replies on Twitter when I asked, "How do you know when a poem is finished?"

50 endings with no epiphany

50 New Year's resolutions re: longing!

50 times I smooshed my face into my dog's wet snout for a kiss

50 times I stalked your social media looking for a disowned part of my shadow

50 ghosts that look *almost* like some part of me I can't name or sound out (the ache)

50 personal rejections

50 chapbooks by Black men, and yet, we need more

50 times I typed my dad's name into a search field and found nothing

50 Mary Oliver poems

50 Toni Morrison quotes

#50 from *Bluets* starts with this sentence: "The confusion about what color is, where it is, or whether it is persists despite thousands of years of prodding at the phenomenon."

50 postmodern ekphrastic poems that undermine "the concept of verisimilitude itself."

50 self-plagiarisms and/or miraculous repetitions of the self

50 copies of copies (where the forehead becomes an orb or an aura or both but all ash)

50 times I rewrote the same text the same line the same poem the *same–same–same . . .*

50 lines I underlined inside *Catalog of Unabashed Gratitude*

50 lectures, workshops, and prompts I taught from *Catalog of Unabashed Gratitude*

50 times my students taught me something new about *Catalog of Unabashed Gratitude*

50 glimmers when a student says they didn't know poetry could "do this" or "say that"

50 invisible permission slips sparkling in their eyeballs—THAT GLEAM THOUGH

50 titles for a poem after Frank O'Hara, after Roger Reeves, after Ocean Vuong, after Claire Schwartz, after Tanya Olson, after Dean Rader, which reads,

"Not Someday, but Today, I Will Love Tiana Clark"

Delta Delta Delta

I don't know why I joined the white sorority.
We whispered Latin passwords to each other.
We wore white robes and sang to each other.

I don't know where I belong.
And the parties, like "Pimps and Hoes"
inside a rented laundromat with fake hickeys

and scars on our skin and pimp juice
in pimp cups. Look at me: the only Black girl
backing it up to Nelly repeating, *It's gettin' hot*

in here (so hot), so take off all your clothes.
Grinding on washers and dryers. Washers
and dryers with my mom at the laundromat

growing up—my fingertips collecting coins
from in between the slits in the couch. Good
treasure. The performance of being poor.

The performance of playing the other
while being the other. Said Memphis.
Said sloppy weather. Didn't Jeff Buckley . . . ?

Didn't he die here? Drowned in some slack
channel off the Mississippi River . . . swimming
with all his clothes on? Said stay. They said

stay off the streets with the names of presidents.
They said, *That's where all the niggers live.*
Another said, *Memphrafrica.* They laughed.

Not me. What hurts now? That I enjoyed
the pretending. I still don't know who drew
a thick dick on my face with a Sharpie.

Didn't wash off for days: faint phallic outline,
faint papyrus, another weak ghost. That I
were white. That hardware of whiteness.

That equipment. That apparatus.
That privileged machinery   felt good.

Gentrification

I had a dream
                    I was still in that shitty house again
            in East Nashville, or East Nasty as some would say,
                with the racist bumper stickers that read,
                                37207 Over the river
                                and through the hood.

In the dream,
                I hear your father coughing up phlegm, his chest
                                    a wet and broken trombone,
his chest   in that room with all the newspapers, piles of old newspapers,
                your father in his disheveled bed, with his newspaper: sheer,
                and open at the corner,
                    wedges of golden light trying to spray through, dust churning
                steamy particles—the daily shadow play of ink,
                                            and I would sneak past
                                        on the way to the bathroom.

This is your father in his velvet red robe, always a little bit open
                and inappropriate, always his raucous throat slackening
                    mucus from the pockets of his slick esophagus, hocking loogies
                            throughout the shotgun house,

                            and I had never tried cocaine before,
                until you tricked me by sprinkling
        this new drug like dirty snow
                    inside our communal blunt,
                        which you later called a *Heavy Chevy*
        and other men laughed and you laughed and I laughed too,

but I didn't know what was so funny. I didn't know
when something was at my expense. I was the only girl there too.
                                I've always been the only girl there
            inside a house with men, being duped by men, waxing their backs

in the middle of the night or lying on my stomach, pretending at pleasure

                                        and calling that pleasure too.
                In the corner,
                a crumbling stick of Nag Champa,
                glowing at the tip like a nipple laced
                with lava, disintegrating—I became a single wisp.

Remember when you called out of work
        because you said the sex was *that good*, but I don't even remember
                what your penis looked like, just that it felt obnoxiously big

like the neck of a giraffe. Have you ever seen two giraffes fight over a female…
fight to fuck? It's wild.

                        Your house, I mean our house for a couple of months,
                has been remodeled, the whole neighborhood gentrified
                except for that dumpy gas station up the road

where we sometimes bought lottery tickets and Cheetos in our pajamas, scratching
                at our luck with orange dust gunked up under our fingernails,
                and I don't remember your chest
                        exactly, only that when you touched me, I shuddered.
Remember
        when you placed Tater Tots on my tongue
        one by one   like a priest from Sonic

and then called me fat after I finished them all—

                                like a *good girl*, you said.
                        I've always wanted to be a good girl,
and then we did whip-its in the back seat
        of some faceless person's car. I can still hear the canisters
                of nitrous oxide clinking and rolling around our feet, quaking
        like little steel ducks as the car turned and turned everything foam,
a seemingly endless loop of right turns on Briley Parkway,

                                a concrete circle hovering

over the city anyway.

I don't recall the fight we had later that night,
                    because that early aughts summer
there was always a party in someone's backyard full of sticks
                                        I wanted to break
                    against the bark of some awkward tree
                    and there was always a party
          with people who did not seem to love me
or themselves and no one knew how to make a decent drink.

I was outside and it was good giant-baseball-stadium-night weather
          and the smear of streetlights struck me
                    as I was trying to break up with you.
                              I was always trying to break up with you
          that summer and you wouldn't let me
          as you grabbed the crotch of your khaki shorts
broadcasting to the dogwoods, *Thank you for the busted nut!*
                    Which at the time I did not understand.
I didn't know about the hard heel of shame   but I do now.

My body made your body explode. So what?

          But I just kept laughing
                    as I drunkenly bit your lips, giggling about ball sacks,
              jealously singing about flying squirrels jumping
                         from branch to branch—they knew how to land
                              on what they wanted with such swagger.

I draped my body over beautiful girls, whispering in their ears, for anyone,
                    anyone to take me home. *Please.*

I don't know where I end. I don't know where I ended up that night.
          The memory is garbled, appears in flashes,
                                        then poof—

I stopped laughing and talking so fast,

> but the hem of grief slipped through
> as I passed our old house, it looked bright
> and brand-new, new porch and everything.

I used to grasp at white men for attention,

> but I don't do that anymore.

There is still a vulnerable part in my neck
that needs clutching,

> but I don't plead anymore.

Scorched Earth

after Kara Walker's *Buzzard's Roost Pass*

Black breasts split within a Civil
War battle-scape. Black breasts hewn

and hacked off like discs of licorice
butter patted over a field of white men at war.

Sherman's army penetrating Georgia.
Sherman marching to Savannah,

not giving a shit about slaves.
Does anyone know where a Black woman

is and is not the linguistics of a landscape:
raped, mastered, controlled, conquered, hoed, mined,

fucked? Kara, why did you cut her up
like that? Kara, you be knowing

how the Blacky body becomes
and is becoming the violent earthwork

of shadow and fissure, such discrepancy
of ink, and I'm looking at your black silk

screen thinking about the repetition
of drinking black milk in Paul Celan's

"Death Fugue," and the line, *we scoop
out a grave in the sky where it's roomy to lie . . .*

Kara, have you read this poem? Kara,
what about that torn forearm above the frame

reaching back in the negative space?
Her head stippled with cannon bursts, cut

flower bombs piercing the profile, dead
silhouette. Kara, would you still not answer me

if I asked you about longing? About your process?
I get so tired when people ask me about this one

poem that I wrote. The truth is: I lied.
Did I have to be there for it to still hurt me?

Am I allowed to conjure the possibility of pain
to protect myself from the pain? Imagine

the shape of my trauma like blacker breasts
pointing in different directions across the gorge

(of my partly   disembodied   body).

Did it have to happen for it to be true?
The truth is: I *felt* like I heard it.

The truth is: I still pull away from my lover
in public. That's my real life. I don't trust

affection. I don't know who's looking
and not looking at me. I don't know

who is going to read this either, but I want
them to like me. Kara, I want you to like me.

For that to happen, should the poem
end with my hand reaching for you too?

Should the poem end with you touching
my black beasts? Whoops, I meant breasts!

Sorry. Oh, sorry for saying sorry so much.
Do you still want to touch my blackest

breast after I've apologized? And let's say
I keep apologizing and then I make

this mistake again . . . will you still want
to touch me? Do you want to see me

touch me? Sometimes, I touch myself
because I don't know if I exist. Once,

a white guy in high school asked to see
my *brown beauties*, kissed my chest for hours.

I didn't want to do it, but I did it,
and I've done that so many times.

Does that make my breasts powerful
or fierce or political or, or . . .

is there anything new they want to say
about the art of Black femmes?

If so, will you say it now? I'm exhausted
and bored by this list of lazy adjectives.

Say something new and then shoot me
in the face three times, or better yet, hang

me in my own cell and say I did it. I dare
you. I double-dog dare you. Do it—do it!

No one will believe that I was murdered.
Do it. Kill me. No one ever trusts a Black

woman's mouth. Kara, what that mouth do
in that lithograph stuck inside a locked room?

Singing stratocumulus clouds—I guess
the weather 'bout to change. Oh, I see

one fang in her mouth. I got sharp teeth
like that too. I leave a mark when I bite

myself. I draw black blood and paint myself,
my Black bitch head over my Black bitch history.

When I was little, I prayed to God for tig ol' bitties,
but they never came, instead I've got small boobs

and large areolas that I've just now stopped
being ashamed of. It's important to be specific

when you ask God to win the war or who's
gonna win the war. Which side? All the same

when the war has always been your body
on the brink—I love my Black breasts! I love

my black breasts! I love my Black breasts!

III.

SOME SCARS
YOU GRAZE

Broken Ode for the Epigraph

. . . who gave me / permission to be this person . . .

—ERIKA L. SÁNCHEZ

O, intertextuality.
O, little foyer to my poem.
O, little first and foremost.
My amuse-bouche, meaning *mouth amuser*,
a little glimpse of the meal to come. And if I could,
I would add an epigraph over everything. Wait . . . who says
I can't? I've always been too much, and I am just now
beginning to cherish this too muchness booming late Baroque/
rococo in my chest (little shells of scattered light decorating
the caves in my poems). I wish people came with little epigraphs
tacked on their foreheads, a little foreshadow couldn't hurt.
I wish fruits had a few ripe lines above their PLU numbers,
a little sneaky peeky of the pulp to come.
O, little cup holder for my quotes.
I love how you hover over the house
of my poem like a cloud from another
book or a bite from another lover, a way
to say I *just* couldn't help myself here. See, I cut
out these lines for you like fuzzy flower stems, severed
at an angle, and they were briefly dead until I placed
them in a vase on top of my poems, prolonging
their life again (such moxie!), because if anything
the epigraph is a little clay container of water
and I placed these blossoms in a vase of life juice
because you are visiting the home of my poem
and I want you to feel special and I think fresh-cut
flowers might make people feel sacchariferous, at least
they do for me, especially when my mother-in-law walks

barefoot into her gorgeous garden and snips the long, lit
stems from the sun-bursting forsythia bush even though
we haven't talked in months, even though I wrote a poem
about her that hurt her, a poem that started with an epigraph
from Natasha Trethewey, and we talked about it
over email and then over coffee and then there was . . .
forgiveness (both sides) and that was it—see: the flowers.
I've always deeply loved Natasha Trethewey's work,
because her parents are like my parents (Black mom,
white dad), another type of epigraph, right? Do you
understand what kind of permission that releases inside
of me? Do you understand how cellular and specific?
Sometimes it's important to know about the blood
before the poem starts. Who makes up these rules
about procedure anyway? I come from clutter. I feel safe
under that little liminal space below the title (underneath
the stairs!) and before that first line. Toi Derricotte
writes, "I am not afraid to be memoir." Yes!
I feel a great affection for Toi Derricotte, because
she has a similar first name as my grandmother,
but spelled differently (Toy), and also because
she drew her beloved dead fish, Telly,
in my copy of *The Undertaker's Daughter*,
writing *Telly Loves You* with the bubbles and
everything! Well, then I am not afraid to be
the epigraph, damn it! I am joyfully trying
to break every rule about poem making
that I know. I want to wake up and like myself
more. I want to wake up and like myself
more. I want to wake up and like myself
more and believe it each time I repeat it.

I want to revel in my poems the way Donika
Kelly does. Have you heard Donika talk
about her poems? Do it—absolute pleasure.
I want more of that giddy precision. I want
to wake up and address myself like the badass
motherfucking epigraph that I am. Hello, epigraph!
I am beginning my body before my body begins.
I want to start my day with somebody else's words.
For example, this morning I started with Ross
Gay's *The Book of Delights* and I keep grinning
and underlining words like "delight radar"
and "delight muscle" and that image of stacking
delights like pancakes and I can hear Ross's
voice as I read them, his joyous timbre
sing-shouting inside these smile-inducing
sentences, which linger over the blue length
of my day (and I just got back from AWP
in Portland, where I heard José Olivarez say
"Lean into length" on a panel about poetry
podcasts. I wrote it down and underneath
his words scribbled: *possible epigraph?*).
Epigraph—a little foreplay, a little playful forest
(I'm safe now, so I can play), a little forecast
of my mood and tone, a little incantation,
little wordy satellites in the white spaces orbiting
the sky parlor of my poems. Epigraph, my father.
Epigraph, my father I've never met, I meet
and let him go at the beginning of every poem
that I write. And isn't loss perpetually dripping sap
from the injured trees bruised or cut in our knuckles
as we write? Sticky sap spilling from the wound,

pitching to survive the bites. And aren't we all writing
the same damn poem over and over again anyway?
Didn't Jack Spicer allude to that once while translating
Lorca? I want to go back to that first epigraph.
The easy association would be God, right? Like this:
so God coos above the waters of the pre-world,
scanning over all that gooey potential, a bajillion
possibilities, millions of us already there, little epigraphs
in the making, gleaming in that first sentence-struck light,
the imperative big bang of God's never-ending breath—

But . . . but what if
        that first epigraph wasn't so spectacular?

What if   it was just someone messaging me
on one of those *spit-in-a-tube* DNA ancestry sites,

saying   that they're my second cousin,
saying   they know how to get in touch

        with my dad

saying   that they gave him my number and email address,
saying   that they told him   I didn't want or need

any   money,   but how
he still
                never
                    reached out?

My daddies have voices like bachelors,
like castigators & crooners . . .

Daughter, you make me shudder, make music of my bones, don't you?
Yes, like castanets. The best blood of my blood, soft blood, boiled

blood of not knowing, bright blood is still in you now, blushing
scarlet cells blossoming in your face, plasma rich as juicy figs, cut

open & gleaming. Muscling that dark abyss, I am the jumbo starfish
skimming & slurping the wounded, deep seafloor. To get close

enough—I came to Nashville once. I wanted to feel the friction
& fiction of having a daughter there. I watched you working

at the restaurant near the replica of the Parthenon with the massive
statue of Athena burning hot & fat & gold inside like a secret sun.

I didn't sit in your section, but near it. I saw your almond eyes
(my eyes). I saw your nose (my nose). The pressure of my face

in your face, barometric. The first words I could not gather
were on your cheeks, passerines perched on telephone wires,

soundless black ovals & lines like unsung musical notes on a scale.
I said nothing as you passed by swaying dirty martinis in your hands,

aglow like a censer, perfume of blue cheese & briny olive juice, murky
as the memory, strained as the jade distance between us. I was the last

guest at the bar, still pushing my slick steak across the white china,
knife clinking, carving the wet meat into smaller pieces of meat: dark

animal juice, gristle tug, tough then delicate tearing—I was stalling.
I didn't want to eat it. I didn't want another reason to get up & leave

you. You walked by me again, I whispered & mouthed slowly: *olive juice.*
Didn't you watch my greasy lips as I said it? Almost looked like I said it,

huh? Dear Daughter, say it in the mirror & that's me saying it, okay?
Would that, could that mouthing (of silent love or persona love

or mimetic love or epistolary love, or your-pain-is-misplaced-here
kind of love, even the dinging repetition of daddyless love

or any kind of damn love-love) ever be enough? Or I didn't know
how to finish this poem, love, & I've been editing it for years, love,

until Jessica Jacobs made me rip it up, love, across a table until I could
see the scaffolding, until I could see the secret of my poem, love, which

is—father, daughter, reader, lover—I don't have to tell you everything.

A Louder Thing

for Kenneka Jenkins and her mother and my mother

What is it about my mother's face, a bright burn
when I think back, her teeth, her immaculate teeth

that I seldom saw or knew, her hair like braided
black licorice. I am thinking of my mother's face,

because she is like the mother in the news whose
daughter was found dead, frozen inside a hotel freezer.

My mother is this mourning mother who begged
the staff to search for her daughter, but was denied.

Black mothers are often seen pleading for their children,
shown stern and wailing, held back somehow by police

or caution tape—

A Black mother just wants to see her baby's body.
A Black mother just wants to cover her baby's body

with a sheet on the street. A Black mother
leaves the coffin open for all the world to see,

and my mother is no different. She is worried
about seeing the last minutes of me: pre-ghost,

stumbling alone through empty hotel hallways,
failing to find balance, searching for a friend,

a center, anyone, to help me home. Yes.
I've gotten into a van with strangers.

I've taken drugs with people who did not care
how hard or fast I smoked or blew.

But what did I know of Hayden? What did I know
of that poem besides my mother's hands, her fist,

her prayers and premonitions? What did I know
of her disembodied voice hovering over the seams

of my life like the vatic song the whip-poor-will
makes when it can sense a soul dispersing?

Still. My mother wants to know where I am,
who I am with, and when will I land.

I get frustrated by her insistence on my safety
and survival. What a shame I am. I'm sorry, Mom.

Some say Black love is different. Once,
I asked my mother why she always yelled

at me when I was little. She said I never listened
to her when she spoke to me in hushed tones

like a white mother would, meaning soft volume
is a privilege. Yeah, that's right. I am using a stereotype

to say a louder thing. I am saying my mother
was screaming when she lost me in the mall once.

I keep hearing that voice everywhere I go.
I follow my name. The music of her rage sustains me.

Hell's Bells

Wasn't allowed to listen
to secular music. Mother said
it was the devil's music.
Church said Satan was made
of music, glory of the Lord
inlaid in his pipes.

Before he was cast out, pastor
said, Satan led heaven's choir.
Lucifer still sings, pastor said,
& we could hear him
on rock 'n' roll records
backwards, hell-bent & warbled.

Sometimes when I'm bored
I research the Manson murders.
I often think about Sharon Tate's
shredded pregnant body. One night,
I even looked up the pictures. Yes,
of course, it was beyond brutal.

I wanted to see complete damage.
The mess didn't scare me.
Supposedly Sharon screamed
Mother! Mother! Mother!
Mother! Mother! Mother!
before & while they knifed her.

When I said I wasn't scared
I'm not saying I wasn't disgusted.
I'm saying copious amounts of blood
& horror look familiar to me,

maybe *expected* is a better word,
or, rather, that I wanted to be certain

I was alive. Okay, it was about control.

I'm grasping at what I know
& don't know for precise meaning,
even now I think *scare* is not quite right,
which makes me think of Lowell's
wedge-headed mother skunk
inside that empty cup of sour cream.

My first CD was Alanis Morissette.
I listened to her *Jagged Little Pill*
on repeat. I liked that secret song
about her breaking into her lover's house
& dancing in the shower just like the raw root
of any dark sound: desperation.

During the whole song, she repeatedly
asks her lover for forgiveness
just like any long poem saying:
would you forgive me, love, for not being concise,
would you forgive me, love, is what I'm struggling to say,
would you forgive me, love, is all I am ever trying to say.

When my mother found
this silver disc she shattered it
in front of my face, yelling.
I don't remember what.
I just recall the pattern in which
it broke like a loud little web.

I threw the mirrored shards
into the trash with my faces,
sliced & reeling. At church
I wouldn't sing & my mother
would poke me in the arm.
I would try & lift my hands,

hoping to feel something
more than just trying to feel
something holy, a peace
I didn't possess but grieved.
I reached above my head
for some slice of surrender.
How pure & wordless & magical
& vague & replete & blurred

it is to worship anything
at all, I sometimes think,
but God keeps nudging me.
My mother is still yelling at me,
& most of the Manson girls
are now old women professing Christ.
Is this what time does to all believers?
(Makes us heaven hungry, revert back?)

Remember buying a new CD—
I'm still clawing at that plastic crinkle,
my faith in the liner notes,
thanking everybody, even you
& you & mostly you. Yes,
you must believe, most of all,
I'm begging to be saved.

I Stare at a Cormorant

with its waterlogged wings spread open,
drying off on a rock in the middle
of a man-made lake after diving for food,
and it makes me think about wonder
and it makes me want to pry and stretch
my shy arms open to the subtle summer
wind slicing through the park, sliding
over my skin like a stream of people
blowing candles out over my feathery
body, and it makes me think about my
church when I was a kid, and how I
lifted my hands to Jesus, hoping
for surrender, but often felt nothing,
except for the rush of fervent people wanting
to be delivered from their aching, present
pain, and how that ache changed the smell
in the room to money and how I pinched
my face and especially my eyes tighter,
tighter, and reached my hands higher—how
I, like the cormorant, stood in the middle
of the sanctuary so exposed and open
and wanted and wanted so much to grasp
the electric weather rushing through
the drama of it all like a shout
in the believer's scratchy throat.

I don't go to church anymore, but today
I woke up early and meditated. I closed
my eyes and focused on a fake seed
in my hand and put my hands over
my heart to shove the intention inside

my chest to blossom—I'm still stumbling
through this life hoping for anyone or
something to save me. I'm still thinking
about the cormorant who disappeared
when I was writing this poem. I was just
looking down and finishing a line
and then I looked back up—gone.

Virtue Signaling, Wisconsin

You couldn't know this loneliness . . .

—NATALIE EILBERT

My first night in Madison   the air was different—
cool, less sticky. The street   was quiet, weirdly   stagnant.

Our house, a pale yellow.   I straddled   the isthmus,
felt ice chip   between both lakes   like frozen lace.

I'm hyper   visible now,   so seen, so   everywhere, then suddenly
nowhere—so much so, I became   Muzak   to my own face.

Now   I'm being followed   inside a grocery store. Down each aisle,
then back again. Now I'm being   stalked   inside a restaurant.

I switch seats.   But it does not matter.   I feel it all: the eyeballs
of this town scorch   the back of my neck,   skin already darker there.

I want to pluck   all the signs   I see stapled across
these manicured lawns   that read,   BLACK LIVES MATTER.

I don't believe you.   There is a sign you buy because
you want so badly to believe   in what it has to say,

and then there is a sign you buy   because
                              you want others to believe you are brave.

A sign can't save   my life.   You will not spare me.
I watch   as you watch me.   I watch

as my white students watch me.   I watch me   watch me, smaller now
than when I first moved here.   Lost a quarter of an inch,

my doctor said.   Most days   I wait
for the bitter winter to end.   Most days   I wait   for another Black

person to pass me.   Most days   they never come.
Most days I wait   for another Black person   to save me.

We hold the gaze.   We do not smile or lie.   A simple nod
simply   saves my life.

Considering *Roe v. Wade*, Letters to the Black Body

Dear Highest Price, Dear Bear the Brunt & Double
Blow, Dear HeLa Cells Still Doubling, Dear

Disproportionately Impacted. Dear Anarcha
without Anesthesia during Surgery with Sims.

Dear Fannie & the Mississippi Appendectomies
with the *Sick & Tired* Ceaseless Sonnet Crown.

Dear Tuskegee Study of Untreated Syphilis. Dear *Black
American Women Are 3 to 4 Times More Likely to Die*

in Childbirth Than White Women. To all the Black Babies
sliced from lynched women's bellies spilling black

jelly then burned as crackled wood singing singe
under silent, white starlight. Dear Unbelieved

Pain. Dear Thick Skin Myth, & Yet, Black Skin
Must Be Thicker. Dear Black Slaves Chewing a Brew

of Cotton Roots as a Form of Reproductive Resistance
Even When Threatened with Death—The Body Strikes.

Dear Alum Water, Teaspoon of Turpentine, Rue,
Camphor, & Chugging Gunpowder Mixed with Sweet

Milk. Dear Black Body That I Adore. Dear Black Body
That I Now Listen to, Shimmering with Acute Tenderness.

Look at my mother's hands. How they search & cut
the thread to take out my weave as if deadheading black

finished blooms from my scalp—what survives in us

is us.

IV.

TO REMEMBER
THE RISK

Broken Sestina Reaching for Black Joy

Yesterday I was smashed with the rush of fresh honeysuckle
from the greenway near my house where I walk every day.
I've been trying to write a poem about buried Black bodies,
but all I want to write about is Black joy and my pleasure
and Black love and Black lives that don't end with viral death,
so I've stopped consuming the news. I've logged off of social

media for a break. Black bodies are buried in the stickiness of history
every day bodies become the next viral death. And yet, each day
I want to write a poem about pleasure. Black pleasure at the root
instead of viral death. What name now? What Black litany? What
Black elegy is repeated on the news? This cycle: Daunte Wright.
I don't know the details yet, because I can't handle the details yet,
but I am mourning him still. This stanza broke the rules. So what?

This stanza will break back inside the form of honeycomb to suck
the lyric into compression, reboot restraint, the grief-joy every day
when I walk around Sylvan Park near a broken track of burned Black bodies,
but all I want to write about is Black joy and *pleasure pleasure pleasure
please* . . . and Black love and Black lives that don't end with viral death,
so I've stopped consuming the news. I've deleted all my social media

apps, but logged back in later, saw your name repeating as death
media. Fresh honeysuckle at dusk smells like sweet earth, ripe bodies,
warm floral notes. Heady with romance and nectar. It permeates the day
I walk over the bridge where I often see a single blue heron, not social,
standing stone-still, stalking Richland Creek fringed with honeysuckle,
which reminds me of any Mary Oliver poem, such pastoral pleasures.

(I'm also still thinking about Claudia Rankine's blossoming blood
list of Black bodies broken from police brutality inside *Citizen*
on page 134. The memoriam fades into the sheer forecast of names

we know will come.) I picked the sestina for its obsessive listing
and twisting. I selected the sestina to probe a problem I can name
but can't answer. The end words are planets orbiting the math.

Pleasure.
Death.
Honeysuckle.
Black bodies.
Social / Media.
Every day.

Every day here are some of the plants and trees I've collected during
my walks. I take pictures on my phone so an app can tell me what they are:
ginkgo, bristly locust, maiden pink, garden star-of-Bethlehem, wild pansy,
birdeye speedwell, eastern redbud, Japanese cherry, apricot, peach,
American holly, beefsteak plant, maypop, common blue wood aster,
Calico aster, eastern white pine, southern sugar maple, scarlet morning glory.

Every day I walk past Dutchman's Curve, the eerie site of the Great Train
Wreck of 1918. Deadliest train wreck in American history, which killed 101
people, mostly African Americans, headed to a factory to make weapons
for World War I. They were stuffed in rickety wooden cars in the front due
to segregation. The front being the most dangerous spot on a train about
to crash, while white bodies were in steel Pullman cars in the back, protected.

But at 100 mph the wooden cars with Black bodies telescoped, splintered,
and caught fire immediately upon impact with another train on the blind curve.
The historian David Ewing describes bodies writhing in pain. Bodies without heads
and limbs. Bodies unidentified, maimed: "The African-Americans that were
on this train did not have a chance to survive, given where they were."

*"The cornfield on both sides of the track was trampled by many
feet, and littered with fragments, of iron and wood hurled from
the demolished cars. The dead lay here and there, grotesquely
sprawling where they fell. The dying moaned appeals for aid or,
speechless, rolled their heads from side to side and writhed in
agony. Everywhere there was blood and suffering and chaos."*

—*THE TENNESSEAN*, JUNE 10, 1918

They asked local butchers to come help manage the gore and horror. Still five
unidentified African American women and three unidentified African American
men destroyed beyond recognition. The railroad masonry abutments remain.
I touched them today.

***

I went on a first date last Thursday. We both leaned into each other's mouths
like two tipped tulips and just kissed each other at a bar called Answer as if that was
an answer—it wasn't. But it was instinctual, sudden, and all pleasure. We kissed
all the way down Murphy Road, walking back to our cars, constellation of our juicy
hands everywhere. We kissed and groped, and I stopped obsessively thinking
about death for a few moments, maybe even for a whole evening, which was

the length of a tercet, an envoi sustained
with pleasure reaching for Black desire,
reaching for the transcendence of pain,   if possible. Is it possible?

Annealing

So what if I keep sniffing her shirt for the commercial scent
of Gain, the one she let me borrow when I slept over her

house and watched her briefly in the morning's vivid fizz
as she slept and sweated out booze from the night before,

the dappled, feral night smeared with dancing and kissing
while dancing. I didn't care who watched us. I didn't care

that I was still married. So what if I was getting divorced.
I watched her as she slept, and I became terrified as we lay

like two torn-off petals, supple and split: me at 35, her at 36,
both of us nearly touching our silk edges—steaming—both

of us wanting and not wanting what the years refused to give
back as leverage. The same decade we each spent with another

lover. The year we met at church as kids: me at 11, her at 12.
Queer question I hid for years. The answer I was afraid

to ask and then ask again—queer candor as in the fulcrum
of desire, the bright seesaw dipping up and down inside

the lacuna of all that aches without subtlety. So close
that I felt a tremendous loneliness there brewing against

my tenderness and sticky breath at her nape. Wait. Or
was it the back of my neck that was buoyantly probing

the erasures? Either way, I failed at reducing the hardness
already blooming and breaking between us like blown glass.

So what if I knew the stress would shatter me. I wanted
to live, even if briefly. So what, I tried ruin for once.

When I Kissed Her Right Breast,
I Became Myself Entirely

Gratitude is black—

—JERICHO BROWN

I wanted to linger at her chest
for hours, study her nipples
through a single-entry point
of appetite, the libidinous latitude
of my longing, but I didn't want
to make it weird, and I kept
thinking of Elizabeth Bishop's
poem again, the one where she's
horrified at these BLACK breasts,
but she also *sees* herself as these
BLACK breasts and she's
overcome by this BLACK
wave and her aunt's all-consuming
scream and the poem zooms out
to World War I and it's February,
which is the month I was born
in Los Angeles in 1984,
and I still admire poems
that fail me and my imagined
BLACK body, and I still want
to talk about Bishop and her panic.
Her awakening. I've taken pictures
of my BLACK, naked body
trying to find traces
of myself (I or you)
there in the waiting room

of my bright, hot breasts—
I touch my BLACK
body and still believe.
I often dared to look!

Indeed Hotter for Me Are the Joys of the Lord

after and for "The Seafarer" and Gabrielle Calvocoressi

I can make a true song
about my body, a ship.
My body, a map
thumbtacked with shame.
Who has the audacity
to take up this much space?
I can make a long poem too
and not say sorry   for me,
myself. I carry myself
like an excuse. I carry myself
constellated with worries.
I say sorry for me,
myself. I carry my borders
like a burden. I carry the borders
of my body like a burdened beast.
But how often have I endured the storm-
driven words of long-winded
white men: hot about my heart,
my house-slave heat?
My mighty thighs burst cobalt
in their reaching and reaching
without completion. Me,
myself, always on the rim
of coming and not coming—
a poem hurts like that, doesn't it?
A familiar frustration:
all that grunting and grinding—
then saying nothing after the peak
animal sounds. But a body has to spill,

right? So I took the pleasure as myself
and touched myself there.
Can I call that God?
Can I, perhaps, want that more
than God? Does God still want me
when I don't want God?
Does God still want me
when I succumb to other gods?
Does God still know my name?
Does God still know my name
when I'm wet and worn
from all that nasty shame,
unzipped by desires
I'm not ready to name?
Last night, I couldn't sleep,
so I raised my hands,
another kind of reaching.
I whispered, *Take this tight sea*
out of the bog in my breast.
My spirit out in the rigid
waterways. The rapid river
lifts for a moment,
and for a moment   I'm freer,
but it all cascades,
everything ricochets back   inside me,
inside my wonky mud drum of body,
booming a thick morass of want.
But can't that be a type of worship too . . .
on my knees? Like a sub?
My mouth gagged with a pink ball
of poems? Getting what I want

and then losing it? Begging
for what I need, but never getting it?
If my body be a long poem
then I want it to go wherever it needs.
I lick dirty verbs in my teeth and feast.
I go back to the buffet with my dirty plate,
because I want my body to say all it has to say
and not be sorry for the saying. Of. It.
I want the long poem of my body
to not apologize for the space it needs
to make and make up. I want to relax
inside a long poem and not feel shame.
Who do you think you are? I repeat.
I am what the long poem says about me.
I am the Seafarer hotter about the Lord,
cold, yet searing with unmet pleasure
and exile, elemental in my suffering.
I want to stop the repetition
that says, *I'm shit—I'm ugly—I'm*
shit—I'm nothing—I'm . . . I'm . . . I . . .
I want to stop the wrist from erasing
my blackety-black-black breasts.
I want to stop my gratitude
from being made a weapon
formed against me and I want this all
from the *not-sorry* long poem
and I want that giant-luscious-deep
wanting to never stop in me.
I want me to not stop me.
Lord, please don't stop.
Don't stop. Get it—get it.

Who do you think you are
without shame? *Enough*.
My body, a pool of pleasures
and my own pleasure first.
I'm done with lying there
clenching from pain, taking pain,
absorbing another person's pain
and calling that pleasure.
My body, a ship, my body
be a long poem, my body
my body without shame,
without shame—
G tells us to draw a map
of how we got here.
G says start anywhere.
G says make a boat
out of paper. G reads
a long poem called "The Seafarer"
while we make the little paper boats.
Little scratches: soft music scrapes
from all the folding and tucking
and folding. Little vessels. Little selves
of our cells. G wants to walk us down
to the lip of fresh water and burn the boats,
but Lake Mendota is frozen over.
G wants to know about the engines
inside long poems. G has a sound
and a symbol. I want a sound
and a symbol, but I'm not ready.
I'm not ready to say what I've always
wanted. I'm not ready to point

at what I so achingly desire
from my body or a lover,
because   it is also   what I fear
most   about me,   is myself.
I'm not ready to know
what that might mean.
I might just need a longer voyage
in this queer body shaking
as it's being named,
called forth and created
from my years of silence,
my years frozen as a little girl
who wasn't allowed
to desire other girls—
I am choosing to mourn
and celebrate her here
in this long poem
that is my body on the brink.
But I still want joy at the end.
I still want to risk joy at the end.
I still want the repetition of joy
at the end. And God. And God
at the end is my joy and my body,
maximal joy, and G is joy and G
makes a "Prairie House" for all of us
and all of us are welcome there.
This is where we have our homes now.
Follow me thither and find belonging
and joy. Our joy. Look how much grief
and gratitude is found in our new city.
My God, what wholeness. G says,

What a lucky sack of stars we are.
Let there be thanks to G and God
at the end. At the end I want
my sound and symbol to be loosened
from snow, Mary Ruefle's "Snow"
to be exact. Her long poem tumbles
after sex and death and birds and sex
but mostly death, because the poem
about sex is mostly about departure:

? I want to start and end from water
? I took my boat to the frozen lake anyway
? I did the ceremony with my bones, bread, and blood
? I laid my questing-boat-body down on the ice
? My long poem is burning
? I set it on fire with my belly
? I blew my breath for the blaze to rise
? I said nothing to my vessel—I said nothing to my vessel
? I said nothing for the rest of the day
? I said my body dipping in the distance

                                   ice-skating through a veil
                                   of white static I watched
                                   until the snow held the body
                                   completely I watched till
                                   I was complete I watched
                                   till I was gone—*Amen.*

Queer Miracle

If I touch her there everything about me will be true.
　　　—NIKKY FINNEY

I've often wondered why Elizabeth Bishop
deleted Alice's blue eyes from the final draft
of her infamous villanelle,

until I was whacked by the bright milky slate
hue of your irises, your petite pitch-black
pupils. They terrified me, not in horror,

but in extreme delight, burning like the talking
bush of God's all-consuming presence, but
without the usual shame I attach to that kind

of precise and piquant glory. I gazed at your
stillness for seconds, because I didn't want
to be destroyed by that simmering node of desire.

I didn't want to be known like that—not yet,
exactly. I didn't want you to see the hidden
pearl of joy in me squished inside the slit

of gooey-oyster darkness, locked with all
my damp and folded expectations. Shuck me.
I've been waiting for the cut, longing for it,

actually—I licked your soft knife, cupped
the intricate lace in your lavender lingerie.
Everything was delicate. Everything pierced

was in repetition: Bishop's iridescent rainbows,
Hass's blackberries, and you. You, the queer
miracle on my couch. It took me a while

to enjoy the revision process, to see that what's
been cut is never lost but found in another
gorgeous form. I once heard Ocean Vuong

say that everything you write is part of the same tree.
I think I know now what led Bishop to this obsessive
fixed form. I milk the tip of that same need and needle,

to slash and then repeat.

***

Anyway, what I think I'm saying is that most of the poem
is just taking out the sopping wet bay leaf.

I Masturbate Then Pray to God

to forgive me I masturbate
then pray to God to forgive me
I masturbate then hate myself
after scrolling endlessly through
porn I never find exactly what it is
that I'm looking for because there is
no category for my type of desire
so I keep searching for a scenario
somewhat sensual not too violent
not too fake with a story some sense
of plot development and I keep clicking
vulgar search terms that never satisfy
I keep working till I master the house
slave kink within me she is looking out
of the window from the big house
across a search field which is my body
on the verge she thinks about running
away but does not dare I'm only here
because one maybe two slaves stayed
resistance isn't always about pushing
back but perhaps submitting to a field
of cotton notating the sublime cottage
cheese color scheme there woven through
brown choking branches like meaty Caucasian
hands clasping dark throats groping thick
brushwork en plein air into the wild gushing
distance with a freer black belly I look like
a human so human my face struck
by artificial light laptop light graphic light
leaking liquid crystals frosted red-green-blue
chromatics throbbing until I pinged until

I rubbed I swiveled racial slurs and curse
words out of my zonked clit arching the ladle
of my lower back by tipping the invective juice
and jive and isn't this how you empty the body's
cup anyway by needling the pleasure buttons
after I scroll through all the porn I masturbate
then pray to God after the shame-hate spiral comes
like a call I deny I send the voicemail to my chest
and never check it but I don't delete it either
as it descends like a zap of divine punishment
smearing some version of God's gloppy guilt
and yes I dislike myself for the hating I dislike
myself for the watching watching another body
wriggle inside another littler window another
torso that is not mine I stand between two
windows as if two mirrors infinitely appearing
into the wild distances splayed by pink pleasure
and bondage where I am the house slave again
wearing an iron muzzle I can barely speak or eat
but I keep slipping little slivers of glass into
my master's food my psyche split by church
and salt I'm praying for God to forgive me
because there is always a moment during my
video-clip-clickbait hole where I see something
that doesn't make me feel quite so good I am
trying to push back on that earlier word *something*
which contains all the effable and ineffableness
of language sure a well-placed placeholder word
can pop but I want to make sure I'm not being lazy
maybe I can try to fetch a metaphor or simile or both
okay so during my video-clip-clickbait hole I search

to find unmitigated pleasure like when I fly I fear
I will die every time and my therapist tells me to accept
this out-of-control fate wave to succumb to the end
not with desire but with focus on my breath I feel immense
joy when I land looking at my survival a warm whispering
I'm alive I'm alive I'm alive I'm alive I'm alive I'm
horny and still waiting to disembark I thank the flight
attendants each one I look inside their eyes as I leave
the long coffin with wings
                              and two quotes
are bobbing around my head right now like two
splish-splashing fish one from Robert Frost,
which I found through Matthew Zapruder's syllabus:

> *What I am pointing out is that unless you are at home in the metaphor, unless you*
> *have had your proper poetical education in the metaphor, you are not safe anywhere.*

And then this excerpt from the beginning
of Robin Coste Lewis's poem "Landscape":

> *Pleasure is black.*
> *I no longer imagine*
> *   where my body*
> *   stops or begins.*

Oh, and this one too (sorry!) from Maggie Nelson
on page 89 from *The Argonauts*:

> *—yet I know I have what it takes to put my body on the line,*
> *if and when it comes down to it; this knowledge is a red hot shape inside me.*

And if you'll allow me just one more quote. I promise
this will be the last and I need to share it because it took me

a long time to find this passage where I've been thinking
about this old man's nasty thumb since college and how it pierced
something (there's that word again) unsettling inside me, another
birthmark on my brain and I can't stop thinking about Heed and Christine
and Christine's puke-stained bathing suit from Toni Morrison's *Love*:

> *It wasn't the arousals, not altogether unpleasant, that the girls*
> *could not talk about. It was the other thing. The thing that made*
> *each believe, without knowing why, that this particular shame*
> *was different and could not tolerate speech—not even in the language*
> *they had invented for secrets.*
>
> *Would the inside dirtiness leak?*

And with that idea of safety and spit and shape and shame
a chorus of *safety spit shape shame safety spit shape shame*
I arrive at the edge of my longing by refusing the unpunctuated
freedom before me I can and can't go further

I close my computer denying myself yet again
my body on the verge yes digital blue-lit throbbing
the house slave kink within me is complicated but freer
as the search field folds in on itself I erase my history

with just one click
no one knows who I really am
I vanish each time
I touch myself.

First Date During Social Distance

Everything wanted to be touched:
my bottom lip, the freshly busted

cherry blossoms, creamy drippings
like soft fluttering pearls that edged

the lack (I meant to write *lake*
but kept the mistake) as I rimmed

the risky desires. And you, you
were all new, suffused with musk

and sadness, height and a milk-
chocolate sweater that curled

at the collar rim, filling out
your shoulders like a ripe demigod.

I forgot about the virus
ravishing the world in its wake.

I forgot about my ache
as the sky dimmed from spring

and wet-paint blue to sherbet
shades of pink fruit juice.

I missed it when the bright
sloppy sun dipped down behind

us and the park slipped right
into that new-new dark as the city

lights lit up like the spangled tips
of hot cigarettes, cooing.

I forgot about the six feet collapsing
between us like prismatic bubbles

breaking between us, between us
the difficult gift (and guilt) of loneliness.

What did it mean to be touched?
It felt like I had never been.

Oops! I hadn't been kissed like that.
That deep and deliberate.

When is the last time someone
wanted to suck and slurp

you up through a straw
from some glad underworld

or some strange netherworld
or any other world

where thousands weren't dying
alone with flooded lungs?

I didn't care who saw us.
I didn't care that I might get sick.

I didn't care—I was such
a reckless, selfish bitch. I know.

You almost walked into the lake,
but I was already drenched,

happy and squealing like a feral pig
inside. *Do you like touching me?*

I kept asking. *You know I do.*
Do you like kissing me?

I kept asking. *You know I do.*
You know I do—stop asking.

Everything wanted to be touched
and I wanted to scratch it all: Him.

My face. My face most of all.
He tenderly bit and tugged

at my bottom lip, and I became
a buoy, bobbing above the hazards.

I slid my index finger in the crack
at the corner of his smile

like a little hook as we licked
and puzzled the need and heat.

Remember the cherry blossoms?
(They're gone now.) So quick

in their delicate beauty
and brief bloom. I remember

I brought a thermometer
in my purse and stuck it

in his mouth like a wet wish—

The Terror of New Love!

for D.

I thought about taking a picture.
To capture what? I decided to live

through the present moment instead:
ephemeral glaze, sentimental risk

with the numb tips of our chilled noses
grazing as we kissed and kissed.

The deep, droning whir of the ferryboat
bloating over Casco Bay, sailing

away from the fringe of Portland, Maine.
It's inside the small, silent slices of time—

right? The terror of new love! The sun-
stung ripples, which made our eyes drip,

refracting and whiting out the landscape
to bright cream as we approached Peaks

Island. Who lives there? We wondered
and imagined as we gasped at the pristine

houses with massive windows perched
along the periphery. Talkless minutes

dotted with intermittent seagulls squawking
overhead. Cold crunch of November air.

Gentle foam frothing and trailing the stern.
It was almost sunset when I leaned back,

softened, and nuzzled deep in the camber
of your embrace, your chest another miracle

of comfort, your arms another possible
home. I wasn't worried about being

too much of myself—yet. In love
again. The first time since the damage

of my divorce. It was gradual, subtly
somatic without the anxiety attached.

You slipped in like a beloved book
or special knickknack that had always

been there, but somehow, I'm just now
seeing it on the shelf stacked and floating

in the part of my heart I'm trying to keep
ajar with a keener warmth. This *it*. Or *itness*?

A gentleness, a personal dispersal, not
of light, but a fresh, odd, familiar feeling—

this blueing calmness not totally erasing
the old fears but welcoming the chance

to try again, to be brave again.

EPILOGUE

But the landscape of devastation is still a landscape.
There is beauty in ruins.

—SUSAN SONTAG

Maybe in Another Life

I think of the kids I may or may not have. I think about
their hair, the possible dark-brown curls. Baby fingers
tapping on my face. I haven't made up my mind yet,
but my body is making decisions before I am ready

to make them. I can't seem to say what it is I want
out loud. I can almost see all my different lives, almost
taste them, like trying to catch the tail end of a cinematic
dream before it evaporates. I want to capture it, a glimpse,

sneak a peek at each distant future before the View-Master
reel clicks. I want to follow the perfume of each life
I could live and linger in it: The vanillas. Milk leaking
from my breasts. Cereal. The piquant odor of parenthood.

The one where I am a mother negotiating happiness.
The one where I am not a mother and still negotiating
happiness, beauty, and rest. Almost 39, and I've never
loved myself more, yet nostalgia wavers all around me

like a montage of mirages muddling memories, complicating
hope, making me miss things I've already mourned.
The bargaining—ain't it a bitch? The bargaining aspect
of grief, to constantly release that which I've already

let go of, but how the water in my mind brings it all back
like the flood current each day, and each morning, in the ebb
I see the seafloor for what it is: another landscape of loss
and renewal, another augur deciphering the tea leaves

in the tide pool revealing the children I might never name,
have, or hold. There is a finite number of eggs and books
inside me. I am trying to release them. I am trying to mourn
the possible futures bursting before me in a fantastic finale

of fireworks, bursting in my mouth like red caviar as I try
to find the right words to say goodbye to little faces I can
only imagine. I'm not sure what I want. Each decision seems
to dissolve at the edge of the beach softened by the watercolor

cream of winter floating above the same shore where Eliot wrote
"The Waste Land" after a mental breakdown a hundred and one
years before me, writing, "On Margate Sands. / I can connect /
Nothing with nothing." I keep looking at the gentle waves

for answers without trying to make another metaphor.
What if the image of what I'm feeling is too heavy to be
carried over into language? Maybe in another life you get
to live out all the lives you've imagined. Maybe in this life

I become who I am by not knowing—

NOTES

"The blues is an impulse to keep the painful details and episodes of a brutal experience alive in one's aching consciousness, to finger its jagged grain, and to transcend it, not by the consolation of philosophy but by squeezing from it a near-tragic, near-comic lyricism. As a form, the blues is an autobiographical chronicle of personal catastrophe expressed lyrically."

—RALPH ELLISON, *LIVING WITH MUSIC: RALPH ELLISON'S JAZZ WRITINGS*

Dear Reader: While writing this book, I kept returning to this quote by Ellison, which was shared with me by Amaud Jamaul Johnson. The possibility of transcending pain permeates these poems.

The epigraph from Aracelis Girmay is from the poem "English Class" in *Kingdom Animalia.*

The epigraph from Rainer Maria Rilke is from the poem "The Dark Hours of My Being," translated by Robert Bly.

I was inspired to write "Self-Portrait at Divorce" after reading *Stag's Leap* again and finally knowing what the hell Sharon Olds was writing about.

"I Like the Way Josh Says Black Love Is Radical" was written during the third or fourth month of the pandemic. It's hard to remember precisely when.

"My Therapist Wants to Know about My Relationship to Work" contains a brief excerpt from Lucille Clifton's poem "birth-day." The affirmations of self-love in "After the Plain Day Becomes Magnificent to Her" were inspired by the teachings of Louise Hay.

"The First Black Bachelorette" contains a reference to the Cardi B song "Bodak Yellow" as well as a line from "Ode on a Grecian Urn" by John Keats. The quote from Hope Oloye is from the *Guardian* article, "Black Students on Oxbridge: 'We Need to Change the Narrative'" by Carmen Fishwick.

The last two lines of this poem are adapted from a sentence in Federico García Lorca's lecture "Play and the Theory of Duende."

"Scattered, Covered, & Smothered: A Southern Gothic Sonnet" is in conversation with the short story "A Good Man Is Hard to Find" by Flannery O'Connor.

References from "50 Lines after *Figure* (2001) by Glenn Ligon" were selected from *A Course in Miracles* and James A. W. Heffernan's *Museum of Words: The Poetics of Ekphrasis from Homer to Ashbery*. The epigraph from Matthew Olzmann is from the poem "Replica of *The Thinker*" from *Contradictions in the Design. Catalog of Unabashed Gratitude* is by Ross Gay.

"Delta, Delta, Delta" features a song by Nelly titled "Hot in Herre."

The line featured from Paul Celan's "Death Fugue" in "Scorched Earth" was translated by Jerome Rothenberg.

The epigraph from Erika L. Sánchez in "Broken Ode for the Epigraph" is from the poem "Saudade" in *Lessons on Expulsion*. This poem also includes a quote from Toi Derricotte's poem "I am not afraid to be memoir" in *The Undertaker's Daughter*.

The title of "*My daddies have voices like bachelors, like castigators & crooners . . .*" is a line from Terrance Hayes's poem "Ars Poetica #789" from *Hip Logic*.

The ending of "A Louder Thing" was previously published in an essay I wrote for *Oxford American* titled "Nina Is Everywhere I Go" (winter 2018 issue). Also, the mention of "Hayden" in this poem refers to Robert Hayden and borrows his interrogative refrain from "Those Winter Sundays."

"Virtue Signaling, Wisconsin" uses the epigraph and first line from Natalie Eilbert's "Reconciliation: Phase I."

"Considering *Roe v. Wade*, Letters to the Black Body" was inspired and driven by research from various sources, but I especially wanted to give credit to Liese M. Perrin's vital article "Resisting Reproduction: Reconsidering Slave Contraception in the Old South."

"When I Kissed Her Right Breast, I Became Myself Entirely" references the poem "In the Waiting Room" by Elizabeth Bishop. The epigraph from Jericho Brown is from the poem "Hero" in *The Tradition*.

"Indeed Hotter for Me Are the Joys of the Lord" was inspired by "The Seafarer," an Old English poem from the *Exeter Book* (tenth century). I used the translation found on Early-Medieval-England.net, where I borrowed the title and one line in my poem, which barreled out of me after I attended Gabrielle Calvocoressi's incredibly illuminating and permission-giving poetry workshop on the "Queer Voyage" in Madison, Wisconsin, on February 2, 2018.

The epigraph from Nikky Finney in "Queer Miracle" is from "The Aureole" in *Head Off & Split*. Oliver Baez Bendorf mentioned this concept of the bay leaf that I adapted for "Queer Miracle," which he heard from Ellen Bass, during a discussion we were having in our shared officed in Madison, Wisconsin, about different revision techniques.

The epigraph from Susan Sontag is from the book-length essay *Regarding the Pain of Others*.

◆　◆　◆

Massive gratitude to the following publications and their editors for their support of my work (sometimes in earlier versions):

The Atlantic—"Broken Sestina Reaching for Black Joy," "Considering *Roe v. Wade*, Letters to the Black Body," and "I Stare at a Cormorant"

"Broken Sestina Reaching for Black Joy" is also published in *The Best American Poetry 2022*, guest ed. Matthew Zapruder, series ed. David Lehman (Scribner, 2022)

Callaloo—"Scattered, Covered, & Smothered: A Southern Gothic Sonnet"

Four Way Review—*"My daddies have voices like bachelors, like castigators & crooners . . ."*

Gulf Coast—"The Hardest Part of the Human Body"

The Kenyon Review—"The First Black Bachelorette"

Los Angeles Review—"Virtue Signaling, Wisconsin"

The Map of Every Lilac Leaf: Poets Respond to the Smith College Museum of Art, edited by Matt Donovan (Boutelle-Day Poetry Center in conjunction with the Smith College Museum of Art, 2020)—"Scorched Earth"

The Massachusetts Review—"Queer Miracle"

Mississippi Review—"Self-Portrait at 35: Terror"

Missouri Review—"Annealing," "*Indeed Hotter for Me Are the Joys of the Lord*," "Self-Portrait at Divorce," and "When I Kissed Her Right Breast, I Became Myself Entirely"

Museum of Modern Art commission—"50 Lines after *Figure* (2001) by Glenn Ligon"

New England Review—"The Terror of New Love!"

The New Yorker—"First Date During Social Distance" and "Maybe in Another Life"

Ploughshares—"Delta Delta Delta"

Poets.org, Poem-a-Day—"After the Reading," "A Louder Thing," and "Proof"

Poetry magazine—"My Therapist Wants to Know about My Relationship to Work"

Sierra Magazine—"I Like the Way Josh Says Black Love Is Radical"

Southeast Review—"Gentrification" and "Hell's Bells"

Tin House Online—"Broken Ode for the Epigraph"

Virginia Quarterly Review—"I Masturbate Then Pray to God"

ACKNOWLEDGMENTS

All my love to my mother (Verna Knight), Papa G-U, my Core Four (Alex Anneken, Ciona Rouse, Jennifer Hope Choi, Lindsay Ambrose), and my Nashville friends near and far. Thank you to my sweet and weird dog, Cooper, who often snored and snarfled under my desk while I wrote many of these poems. Thank you to my walks at the McCabe greenway and Centennial Park, which kept me grounded as I was writing this book. Tremendous thankfulness to Drew Love for his constant support, encouragement, brilliant suggestions, and for daring me to eat the sun.

Heck yes to Maggie Smith, who shared the Rilke quote, which kept me buoyed and hopeful in the aftermath of my divorce. Thank you to Claire Schwartz, who helped me with an earlier version of this book with her brilliant edits and questions. To Amaud Jamaul Johnson for Lorca and Ellison, and for all he did in Madison to keep me sane, supported, seen, and inspired. To Gabrielle Calvocoressi (G), who keeps breaking me open with *gratitude and funk*. To my inspiring and supportive cohort at UW-Madison, Wisconsin (Oliver Baez Bendorf, Leila Chatti, Tia Clark, and Marta Evans), and everyone in our Mutually Assured Vulnerability salon; the freedom of MAV helped me with the genesis of this book and to trust my own voice again. Massive thanks to my amazing therapist, Brenda, who keeps reminding me that I am more important than my work! Lots of appreciation to my incredible agent, Jamie Carr. Thankfulness and admiration to all of my students over the years. I keep learning from you. Thank you for keeping me a forever pupil of poetry.

Thank you for rejection, which taught me patience, the gift of failure, and to resee my own book again and again and again.

My heartfelt appreciation to the following brilliant poets and editors for inspiration, acceptances, and very helpful suggestions for the poems that appear in this book (in no particular order): Joshua Moore, Faith Hill, Phillip

B. Williams, Kevin Young, Hannah Aizenman, Jessica Jacobs, Ross White, David Baker, Gregory Pardlo, Matt Donovan, Adam Clay, Ada Limón, Rigoberto González, Jacob Griffin Hall, Jayme Ringleb, Camille Dungy, Chelsea B. DesAutels, Jennifer Chang, Blas Falconer, Ellen Doré Watson, Charles H. Rowell, Aimee Nezhukumatathil, Don Share, Lindsay Garbutt, Matthew Zapruder, Safiya Sinclair, Eileen Myles, Jericho Brown, Ocean Vuong, and Jenny Xu. Also, a big shout-out to the amazing copy editors at Washington Square Press/Atria/Simon & Schuster! I deeply appreciate your exacting eyeballs and attention to detail.

Immense gratitude for the generous support I've received from the National Endowment for the Arts Literature Fellowship, the Jay C. and Ruth Halls Poetry Fellowship at the Wisconsin Institute for Creative Writing, the Kate Tufts Discovery Award (Claremont Graduate University), Southern Illinois University at Edwardsville, Smith College and the Grace Hazard Conkling Writer-in-Residence, the Sewanee School of Letters, the Sewanee Writers' Conference, and the Amy Lowell Poetry Travelling Scholarship. I also appreciate every reader, school, university, and organization that has supported my work.

Always my endless gratitude for Bill Brown, my first and forever poetry teacher. BB, I will miss you deeply. Your memory, a continual blessing. You changed my life at fifteen years old. I am the poet I am today because of what you taught me. I carry your spirit with me each time I teach. You were the first person to read poems to me. Because of you, I fell in love with Sharon Olds, Rita Dove, and Li-Young Lee. You were the first person to truly listen to my poems with your whole body: eyes closed, pulling your ears forward with your fingertips—a gift. You taught me to follow the rhythm in my poems by bringing a metronome to class. I continue to carry that click with me whenever I write.

Thank you, thank you, thank you!

ABOUT THE AUTHOR

TIANA CLARK is the author of the poetry collection *I Can't Talk About the Trees Without the Blood* (University of Pittsburgh Press, 2018), winner of the 2017 Agnes Lynch Starrett Poetry Prize, and *Equilibrium* (Bull City Press, 2016), selected by Afaa Michael Weaver for the 2016 Frost Place Chapbook Competition. Clark is a winner of the 2020 Kate Tufts Discovery Award (Claremont Graduate University), a 2019 National Endowment for the Arts Literature Fellow, and the winner of the 2015 Rattle Poetry Prize. She is a recipient of the 2021–22 Amy Lowell Poetry Travelling Scholarship and 2019 Pushcart Prize. Clark was the 2017–18 Jay C. and Ruth Halls Poetry Fellow at the Wisconsin Institute of Creative Writing. She is the recipient of scholarships and fellowships to the Bread Loaf Writers' Conference, Sewanee Writers' Conference, and Kenyon Review Writers Workshop. Clark is a graduate of Vanderbilt University (MFA) and Tennessee State University (BA), where she studied Africana and women's studies. Her writing has appeared in the *New Yorker*, *Poetry* magazine, the *Atlantic*, the *Washington Post*, *Virginia Quarterly Review*, *Tin House* Online, *Kenyon Review*, *BuzzFeed News*, *American Poetry Review*, *Oxford American*, *The Best American Poetry 2022*, and elsewhere. She is the Grace Hazard Conkling Writer-in-Residence at Smith College. During the summer, she teaches at the Sewanee School of Letters.

Clark is currently working on *Begging to Be Saved*, a memoir-in-essays reckoning with Black burnout, millennial divorce, faith, art making, and what lies on the other side of survival, which sold to Jenny Xu at Washington Square Press/Atria.